Portugal

An Illustrated Journey for Young Explorers
Discover the Rich Geography, History, and Culture of Portugal

Visit our author page for more children's books
Amazon.com/author/88

By Nicole Damon

Introduction: Welcome to Portugal! A Country of Adventure and Wonders

Hello, young explorers! Are you ready to embark on an exciting journey? Today, we're going to discover a magical land called Portugal. It's a country filled with colorful traditions, delicious food, and breathtaking landscapes. So, pack your imagination, and let's dive into the wonders of Portugal!

A Land of Explorers and Discoveries

Portugal is a small country in southwestern Europe, but don't let its size fool you. It has a big heart and an even bigger history! Long ago, brave Portuguese explorers like Vasco da Gama and Ferdinand Magellan set sail across the unknown seas. They discovered new lands and connected the world in ways never imagined before. Because of their adventurous spirit, Portugal is often called the "Land of Discoveries."

A Country of Contrasts and Beauty

Portugal is a land of contrasts. In the north, you'll find lush green valleys and ancient castles. In the south, there are sunny beaches with golden sands and clear blue waters. The country is also home to beautiful islands like Madeira and the Azores, each with its own unique charm.

A Celebration of Culture and Traditions

Portuguese culture is a vibrant tapestry woven with music, dance, and festivals. Have you ever heard of Fado music? It's a soulful style that tells stories of love, loss, and longing. And if you visit Portugal in June, you'll witness the streets come alive with colorful decorations and lively parades for the popular Saints' Festivals.

A Taste of Portugal

One thing you must not miss in Portugal is the food! Portuguese cuisine is a delicious blend of seafood, spices, and sweets. Imagine tasting the famous pastéis de nata, a creamy custard tart that melts in your mouth, or savoring a plate of bacalhau, a traditional codfish dish.

An Invitation to Adventure

So, are you ready to explore Portugal with us? There's so much to see, learn, and taste in this enchanting country. From its historic cities to its stunning landscapes, Portugal is a treasure chest waiting to be opened. Join us on this journey through land and culture, and let's uncover the secrets of Portugal together!

Where in the World is Portugal?

Welcome, young adventurers! Today, we're going to take a closer look at where Portugal is on the map and discover the amazing landscapes that make this country so special. So, grab your compass and let's set sail on a journey to find Portugal!

Location on the Map

Imagine you're looking at a map of the world. Can you find Europe? Great! Now, look towards the western edge of Europe, right next to Spain. That's where you'll find Portugal, a small country with a big heart. It's like a hidden gem, waiting to be explored!

A Walk Through History

Are you ready to travel in time, young explorers? Today, we're going on a walk through history to uncover the amazing stories of Portugal's past. From ancient settlers to daring explorers, let's discover how Portugal became the country we know today!

Early Settlers: Celts and Romans

Long, long ago, before Portugal was even called Portugal, it was home to different groups of people. The Celts were one of the early settlers. They were known for their bravery and love of nature. They built hill forts and left behind beautiful jewelry and pottery.

Then came the Romans around 200 BC. They brought with them roads, bridges, and cities. Have you heard of the Roman Empire? Portugal was part of it! The Romans introduced new farming techniques, and the country became famous for its olive oil and wine.

Age of Discovery: Explorers like Vasco da Gama

Zoom ahead to the 15th and 16th centuries, an exciting era called the Age of Discovery. During this time, brave explorers set out on thrilling adventures to uncover new lands and navigate uncharted seas. Portugal was at the center of it all! Brave explorers like Vasco da Gama set sail into the unknown to find new lands and sea routes.

Vasco da Gama's most famous voyage was to India. He sailed around the tip of Africa, called the Cape of Good Hope, and reached India in 1498. This was a huge achievement because it opened up trade routes and brought spices, gold, and other treasures back to Portugal.

Modern Times:
Becoming the Portugal We Know Today

After the Age of Discovery, Portugal went through many changes. It had its ups and downs, like all countries do. In the 20th century, Portugal became a republic, and in 1974, it had a peaceful revolution called the Carnation Revolution. This helped Portugal become the democratic and vibrant country it is today.

Regions and Geography

Portugal is full of natural wonders, with each region having its own beauty. In the North, you'll find green mountains and the Douro Valley with its vineyards. The Center is home to Serra da Estrela, the highest mountains in mainland Portugal, great for hiking and skiing. The South has the Algarve, known for its sunny beaches and cliffs. Portugal also has islands like Madeira and the Azores, with tropical forests and wildlife.

Climate: Sunshine and Seasons

Portugal has sunny weather and mild seasons. In spring, the countryside is colorful with blooming flowers. Summer brings sunny days and warm weather, perfect for beach fun. Autumn has cooler weather and golden leaves, ideal for walks and city exploration. Winter can have snow in the North but is milder in the South, making it a cozy time to visit.

Celebrating Culture

Hello, young adventurers! Today, we're exploring Portuguese culture. In Portugal, people speak Portuguese, a beautiful language that sounds like music. They love to celebrate with festivals like Carnival, where everyone dresses up in colorful costumes and dances in the streets. There's also Saint Anthony's Day in Lisbon, where the city smells of grilled sardines, and the Feast of Saint John in Porto, where people have fun with fireworks and gentle taps from plastic hammers.

Music and dance are important in Portugal too. Fado is a special kind of music that's full of emotion, often about the sea and love. In different parts of Portugal, you can find traditional folk music and dances, where people wear bright costumes and move to the rhythm of guitars and tambourines. Portuguese culture is all about joy, traditions, and bringing people together. What part of Portuguese culture would you like to experience?

Delicious Delights

Hello, young food explorers! Today, we're tasting some yummy Portuguese dishes. Let's start with bacalhau, the king of Portuguese cuisine. It's dried and salted codfish that can be cooked in many ways, like grilled or baked. Another favorite is pastéis de nata, little custard tarts that are crispy outside and creamy inside, sprinkled with cinnamon and sugar.

Portugal is also famous for its seafood, thanks to its long coastline. In the summer, grilled sardines are a popular treat, often served with bread and olive oil. Another seafood favorite is cataplana, a stew with clams, shrimp, and fish.

And we can't overlook the treats! Almond cakes from the Algarve are soft and flavorful, while honey bread from Madeira is gooey and sugary, a perfect match for a cup of tea.

Magical Places to See

Welcome back, young adventurers! Today, we're going to explore some of Portugal's most magical placcs. From bustling cities to breathtaking beaches, let's discover the wonders of Lisbon, Porto, and the Algarve!

Lisbon: The Capital City with Trams and Towers

Lisbon, the capital of Portugal, is a city full of charm and history. Here are some highlights:

•**Trams**: Hop on one of Lisbon's iconic yellow trams and ride up and down the city's hills. Tram 28 is especially famous for its scenic route through historic neighborhoods.

•**Belém Tower**: This beautiful tower by the river was built over 500 years ago to protect the city. It's like a fairy-tale castle with its turrets and battlements.

•**Jerónimos Monastery**: A stunning example of Manueline architecture, this monastery is a masterpiece of stone carvings and intricate details. Don't forget to try a pastel de nata from the nearby bakery!

Porto: Famous for Its Exquisite Wine and Vibrant Houses

Next, let's travel to Porto, known for its wine and vibrant buildings:

•**Ribeira District**: Wander through the narrow streets of the Ribeira, with its colorful houses and lively atmosphere. It's like stepping into a painting!

•**Port Wine:** Porto is known around the world for its Port wine, which is a special kind of wine that's sweet and rich. It's often enjoyed as a dessert after a meal. When you visit Porto, you can explore wine cellars where Port wine is made and stored. These cellars offer tastings, so you can try different types of Port wine and find your favorite. It's like going on a delicious adventure in the world of wine!

•**Dom Luís I Bridge**: This impressive metal bridge spans the Douro River, connecting Porto to Vila Nova de Gaia. The view from the top is breathtaking!

Algarve: Beaches, Cliffs, and Caves

Finally, let's head to the Algarve, Portugal's sunny southern region: The Algarve is famous for its incredible beaches with fine, golden sands and sparkling turquoise waters. One of the prettiest beaches in the whole world is called Praia da Marinha! It's a perfect place to play in the sand, splash in the water, and have a great time under the sun.

• **Cliffs and Caves**: Explore the dramatic cliffs and hidden caves along the coastline. The Benagil Cave is a natural wonder with a hole in its roof, letting in sunlight.

•**Water Sports:** The Algarve is a fantastic and thrilling spot for water sports like surfing, kayaking, and paddleboarding. Whether you're a beginner or an expert, there's an abundance of exciting fun to be had in the sparkling water!

Nature's Wonders

Hello, young nature explorers! Today, we're exploring Portugal's beautiful outdoors. Let's start with Peneda-Gerês National Park, where you can hike in rugged mountains, spot wildlife like deer and wild boars, and see sparkling waterfalls and clear rivers. Then, we'll visit the islands of Madeira and the Azores, known for their lush gardens, dramatic cliffs, and adventures like mountain biking and scuba diving.

Portugal's coastline is also full of treasures. You can relax on beaches with wild waves or calm waters, watch dolphins and whales on a boat trip, and visit lighthouses like the Cabo da Roca lighthouse, which is on the westernmost point of mainland Europe. There's so much to see and do in Portugal's great outdoors!

Sporting Spirit

Hello, young athletes! Today, we're exploring sports in Portugal, where football is a huge deal! It's not just a sport, but a way of life. People of all ages love cheering for their favorite teams, and football matches are full of singing and flag-waving. Portugal has famous players like Cristiano Ronaldo, one of the greatest footballers ever! The rivalry between big teams like FC Porto, SL Benfica, and Sporting CP makes football matches super exciting.

But there's more to sports in Portugal than just football. Surfing is big too, with great spots like Nazaré and Ericeira for catching waves. Nazaré is known for some of the biggest waves in the world! Portugal also has other popular sports like athletics, cycling, and basketball. The Volta a Portugal is a famous bike race through the country's beautiful landscapes. No matter what sport you like, there's something for everyone in Portugal!

Economy and Innovation

Hello, young explorers! Today, we're learning about Portugal's economy and innovation. Portugal is famous for its agriculture, producing cork from cork oak trees, delicious olive oil from olive trees, and famous wines like Port from the Douro Valley. But that's not all! Portugal is also growing in industry and technology, making high-quality textiles and becoming a hub for tech startups and new inventions. Plus, Portugal is a popular tourist destination, with beautiful beaches, historic cities, and friendly people who love to share their culture and traditions.

Portugal Today and Tomorrow

Hello, young explorers! Today, we're looking at daily life in Portugal. Kids there start school at six years old and learn subjects like Portuguese, math, science, and English. After school, they have time for homework and play. Adults work in different jobs like in offices, shops, or tourism, and everyone loves spending time outdoors, at the beach, in parks, or playing sports. Families and friends often get together to celebrate and have fun.

Looking ahead, Portugal is excited about the future. The country is working on new ideas and technology to keep growing and creating opportunities. They also care a lot about the environment and are using more renewable energy to keep Portugal beautiful and healthy. Most of all, people in Portugal dream of a future where everyone can live in peace and harmony, believing in the power of community to build a bright future for everyone.

Visit our author page for more children's books,
and remember to follow us for updates on new releases,
including illustrated storybooks, biographies,
fun-fact books, coloring books for kids, and more:
Amazon.com/author/88

Nicole Damon

+ Follow   ⓘ   HOME   ABOUT   ALL BOOKS

Quick look

for Kids: A Child's Guide to the Wonders...

Kindle Edition

$0⁰⁰ kindleunlimited

Other formats: Paperback

Quick look

for Young Explorers : Discover the Rich...

Part of: Illustrated Countries of the World for...

Kindle Edition

$0⁰⁰ kindleunlimited

Other formats: Paperback

Quick look

Children: Dreaming Big, Reaching for the...

Part of: Illustrated Biographies for Children (12...

Kindle Edition

$0⁰⁰ kindleunlimited

or $2.99 to buy

Other formats: Paperback

Quick look

Easter Golden Egg Adventure: A Story of...

Kindle Edition

$0⁰⁰ kindleunlimited

or $2.99 to buy

Other formats: Paperback

Made in the USA
Monee, IL
20 May 2025